The **Oldie**
BOOK OF CARTOONS

'I can't really talk now. I'm being chased by a bull'

The *O*ldie
BOOK OF CARTOONS

A NEW SELECTION

Chosen by
Richard Ingrams

Published by Oldie Publications Ltd, 2013

65 Newman Street, London W1T 3EG
www.theoldie.co.uk

Copyright © 2013 Oldie Publications Ltd

ISBN: 978-1-901170-21-4

A catalogue record for this book
is available from the British Library

Printed in the UK by Butler Tanner and Dennis Ltd

Introduction

'All cartoonists are geniuses,' wrote the novelist John Updike, who worked for the *New Yorker* in his youth. Geniuses they certainly are but their achievements are seldom given the recognition they deserve.

As an editor who spends a good deal of his time happily leafing through their submissions, I like particularly the variety of styles. Some cartoonists are skilful artists, others are 'primitives', but they are all of them uniquely different. You can seldom detect a cartoonist consciously imitating another cartoonist.

I admire, too, the skill and inventiveness with which they continue to make original jokes about the traditional subjects – people marooned on desert islands, suicidal businessmen on the window ledge, hen-pecked husbands, etc. Luckily the mad world in which we live today is providing a quantity of new targets, especially in the realm of technology – computers, mobiles, Kindles – all of them becoming more sophisticated day by day.

I would like to thank the cartoonists, all listed at the back of the book, for providing me and readers of *The Oldie* with so many very welcome laughs.

RICHARD INGRAMS
July 2013

'We've been asked to investigate a report that a large dog is causing trouble in the district'

'So much for Google – there's nothing about
hiring contract killers!'

'I think I need some "me-time"'

'Right, Sid – programme the satnav for Brighton'

'Oh, come on, all I did was forget the milk, I didn't need a flippin' lecture'

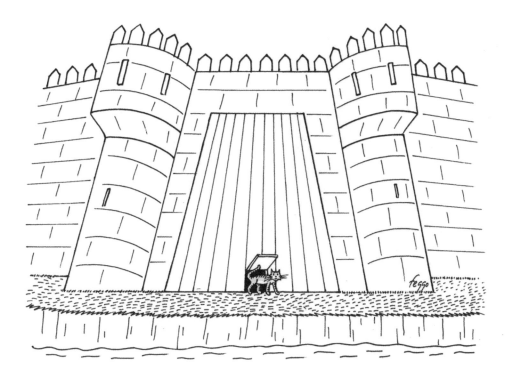

'Would you like Mummy to download a
bedtime story to your iPod?'

'...and you have two minutes on your chosen subject, "The life and times of Christine Keeler"'

'To be honest, the whole of March is a bit of a no-go'

'He's tunnelled out!'

'So you're his fancy woman!'

'I've got the English blues... Still, mustn't grumble...'

'We realised that the "Swimming with Dolphins" thing was over...'

'And don't forget to act rich'

'Who plumbed this in?!'

'Say "Arrrrrr, Jim lad"'

'Can Johnny come out?'

'Good of them to find us a table'

'It's funny – everyone always remembers where they were when Humpty Dumpty had a great fall'

'God sees and knows everything – like Google with a beard'

'He's doing his out-of-work experience'

'Take a letter, Brother Francis – "Dear Father Sebastian..."'

you Are not the Only gAy iN The VILLAOE

'You're not taking the microwave are you?'

'This year, next year,
not any time soon, whenever'

'...and we're not expecting any nonsense about a grossly disproportionate response'

'Are you sure there isn't, Edith?'

'Well, I still don't know where we are'

'Frankie – you're not supposed to see me on our wedding day'

'When I grow up I hope to be an iconic example of the misspent life'

'Haven't I seen you on television?'

'They keep laughing at us. Bastards'

'I'll call you back –
just ticking some boxes'

THE BRITISH
WEIGHTWATCHERS
ANNUAL
BALL

DANCING TO
THE
GASTRIC
BAND

'Go to sleep dear, or the childcare
professionals will come and get you'

'The obese one on the end can't possibly be Famine...'

'Sorry there's no food. We were kind of hoping you'd bring some'

'No one leaves the class until I find out who's responsible for this'

'We'd like a little boy for our dog'

'Peace in our time!... Yet another victory for common sense and
diplomacy over mindless violence and brutalism'

'How many times, Mother?
Badger baiting is illegal'

Your Father and mother are not married

'...but I'm not sure about this proposal to burn our whalebone corsets'

'Good news, Lord Cardigan – you're going to get a bonus!'

'It's getting more and more difficult
to be smug middle-class'

'Well at least he's not sitting at home scrounging off the government, darling'

'Where do you see yourself in five minutes' time?'

'You complete bastard!!'

'Seven 'A's – I'm sure these tests are getting easier'

'There's a Saint Barbie?'

'You have the right to remain silent'

'Have you considered opera?'

'Hmm, impressive CV'

'We tend to favour more traditional forms of anaesthetic here'

'Why don't you just get a mobile phone? Then people won't think you're weird'

'My wife thinks I'm on a date with a hot piece'

'Don't bother with the box – I'll be running out of the shop without paying'

'Think Afghanistan... This is a conflict you cannot win'

'Your ideas are outstanding, Beresford, I'm glad I thought of them'

'I see you haven't eaten here before'

'Yesterday, all my troubles seemed so far away... or was it Tuesday?'

DANGER! SLIPPY SURFACE

H&S EXEC.

HUNTER

SOLVED

UNSOLVED

HUSHED UP

NICK DOWNES

'It's the car park on CCTV.
I missed last night's episode'

'This should counteract your allergic reaction to the antidote to your latest medication...'

MAZURKE

'The thin man inside you who has
always been trying to get out is now
also clinically obese'

'Just my husband – he's either shot
himself or opened another bottle'

'How should I know if they hurt? I ain't kicked anyone with them yet!'

NOT IN SERVICE

'It was assisted suicide'

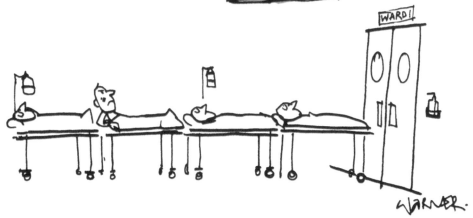

'OMG! They must be Boris Dancers!'

'I wonder if you've considered the pain-tracking phone apps, Mr Arnold?'

*'When the music stops, sit down in the nearest chair.
Whoever doesn't get a chair will be made redundant'*

'I'm just popping next door for
a cup of sugar, Cyril'

'Wii skiing – he tripped over a pouffe'

'The funeral business has been good to me'

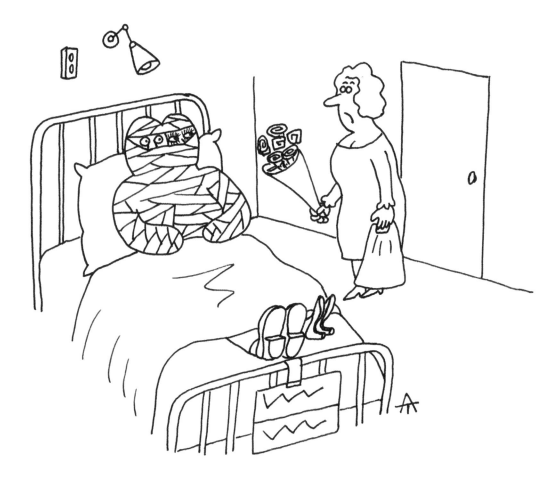

'What do you mean you'd like a shed?'

'Dad, I couldn't sleep, so I hacked into the USA missile system...'

46

'Well you'll think they'll taste like mackerel but they won't'

'I don't know... Where are you going
to keep your mobile phone?'

'We feel the less said about this one the better'

'Ignore it – it's gesture politics'

'I've got sand everywhere'

'Hold on, I need to check my p-mail'

'If only they'd had mobile phones...'

'Whew! That was one hot asexual reproductive act!'

'Cut my hair... and the crap'

'I allowed an element of
complacency to creep into my
game plan and paid the price'

'I forgot my glasses – can you tell me the sell-by date, the best-before date,
the salt content, the e-numbers and the eco-carbon label?'

'We're closed. God is dead'

'Is there a reason my peas are touching the mashed potatoes?'

'A stabbing pain, you say?'

'Look. I'll show you – didn't they teach you anything in school, Grandad?'

'We've been born into a surveillance society'

'Kids today... What do they look like?!'

'Oh for goodness' sake!
Stop celebrating Britishness...'

'Your friends and family are here, Roger, because we can no longer sit idly by and watch you throw your life away on yoga classes'

'If you want to smirk, Roger, go outside'

'I've got two tickets for the Rolling Stones if you're interested!'

'Hang on. I'm pretty sure I can download an app for this'

'Well I suppose when you put it that way...'

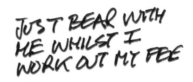

ANY SIGN OF AN ECONOMIC RECOVERY SINCE I ASKED YOU AT THE BEGINNING OF THE INTERVIEW?

TV NEWS

'The buck has stopped here, Miss Palmer. Get rid of it'

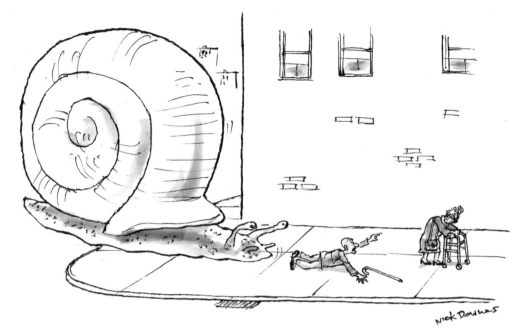

'Go on without me – save yourself!'

'You do realise that that religious symbol
could cause offence?'

LIKE TO DO SOMETHING
INAPPROPRIATE, DEAR?

'I now pronounce you man and man'

'Aren't there any concessions for the elderly?'

'It's for you, Grandad'

'A book on levitation, you say?'

'Well, you've grown old gracefully
– now what?'

'Your mother's got to carry on
working as long as I live'

'What say we change our religion
so you can wear a burka?'

'Thank you for choosing this pavement.
We hope you have had a pleasant journey'

'As a postulant, you will eschew
ostentatious clothing...'

'Do not take this product if you are pregnant or nursing. Talk to your doctor if you have a history of liver disease. May cause headaches, nausea, dizziness and nosebleeds. Check with your primary care provider...'

'This should open a few doors for you'

'I want you to bring out my character'

'...and finally may I ask how satisfied you were with the way I handled your funeral today?'

'I'm afraid I can't discuss individual cases'

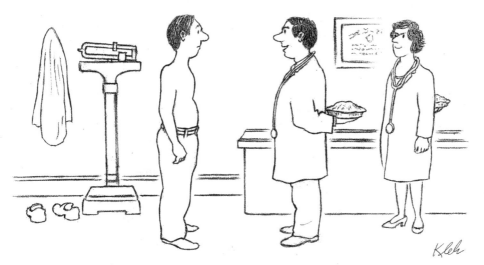

'Around here we believe that laughter is the best medicine'

K.J.Lamb

'No, it's just a piece of plastic –
but it lets me talk to myself without
people thinking I'm crazy'

de la Nougerede

'We're expecting property prices to rise as the available land melts...'

'The Mitchells' costume party – I suppose
you'll be going as a pirate again?'

'Careful! You could put an eye
out with that thing'

'Now, Hopkins – you don't want to have to justify your remuneration to the media, do you?'

'I think I'll join – I've got nothing to lose'

'Jeez, if you're going to cry about it, keep your stupid job'

THE PERSON YOU
ARE CALLING KNOWS
YOU ARE WAITING

'She's allowed to visit him twice a month...'

'Things didn't go exactly to plan –
my husband ran off with the hitman'

"Physick for the cure of thy Ague.'
When was the last time we cleared out
this medicine cabinet?'

AIRPORT CAFE

'Sir, you left your Chelsea bun unattended
and it had to be destroyed'

'Bring desired amount of frozen vegetable to a boil.
Cover. Reduce heat. Simmer five minutes. Serve'

'Night night, sleep tight, don't let the foxes bite'

'Ladies and Gentlemen, we are being held here forever.
We won't be moving shortly or at all. Thank you for your patience'

'Common sense has prevailed'

'He asked for an instant'

'With this ring I thee wed'

'How do you like your tin opened?'

'That's nice, dear – we've received
an incitement to riot'

"I expect you really
miss the kids."

'Before we start, why don't we go round and each say a little something about ourselves?'

'Their lobby is getting stronger'

'Just because your socks seem further away each morning it's not exactly conclusive proof that the universe is expanding'

'This is awkward – I left the glass beads in my other trousers'

'... Finally I'd like to thank my
mother, who's supported me
in every mistake I've made'

'Relax, sir. Just routine'

'Guess he should've opted for the gold watch, eh, Mr Krause?'

'Can't you talk about anything apart from the weather?'

'Everything's "ME-ME-ME" with you people'

'You will be hanged, drawn and quartered... but not necessarily in that order'

'He's a tortured genius – I make sure of that'

'I personally don't want to fire you, Rogers, but Mr Wiggles
feels very differently, don't you Mr Wiggles?'

'Now enter a six in that little box'

'Hang on while I tweet that I'm telling
you to hang on while I tweet'

'I've started, so I'll finish'

'Your vows may be monitored
for training purposes'

'A message to a space shuttle informing them
their engines have failed should not have a
smiley face at the end of it, Mike'

'Gosh, is that the time?'

'Far from being entitled to incapacity benefit, you seem
uniquely qualified for a career on the high seas'

'Derek built his business up from scratch'

'Would sir like to try the wine?'

'Can you support my daughter on
what you pilfer from collection plates?'

'I want a gay divorce'

'...and this is my solicitor'

'You're living in the past, Eric'

'I looked up "ubiquitous".
It just says "Stephen Fry"'

'...and he prefers his bedtime story to be read in a London East End gangster's accent...'

'What would I recommend? Well, Vesuvio's over the road is very good'

'Where can I get one of those wigs?'

'I'm hoping to raise 2,000 turbines this year'

'And how long have you had these
feelings of being abominable?'

'At ease'

'Can I get you anything
from the pharmacy, sir?'

'It's good to get away from the office...'

BILL PROUD

'So you're an out-of-work actor, then?'

'I've got a friend in the magic circle who knows how he does that'

'Why can't you play with your mobile phone like any normal person?'

'We asked the department for an interview
but no one was available'

'Apparently this has had
really bad viewing figures'

'I can feel my depression lifting'

'Here comes a Kindle to light you to bed...'

'What ever happened to "You can't take it with you"?'

'I'm collecting for Christian Aid week'

'Did you pack your own luggage?'

CRY GOD FOR HARRY, ENGLAND AND... ER... WHAT'S THE OTHER ONE?

GEOFF HORTON

'Signal them to cross, and when they're in front of the car, honk the horn'

'Don't just sit there – nick a bike and look for work!'

'Don't let the burnt meatloaf be a metaphor for our marriage, Ed'

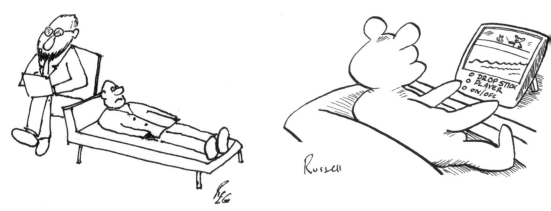

'Why do you want to be a cartoonist?'

'This board needs more diversity. Perkins – get a sex change'

'I can remember when a billion pounds was a lot of money'

'The game's up – they've found the tunnel'

'Gentlemen – I'm declaring a lack of interest'

'Caught anything?'

'I've changed the way I shop'

'Ah, Mozart's "Eine Kleine Liftmusic"'

'See anything?'

'No idea, I'm afraid. I'm not from round here'

'...Semi-colon...'

'Arnold, it's the piano tuna'

'I'm worried about Malcolm –
he's not in a good place'

'All right – tomorrow you can park'

'It's nice to see a bit of honesty
creeping back into banking at last'

'Cramp makes you walk funny – go on, give us a laugh'

'Sorry about this, sir – it's just a
precaution while I do your room...'

'Richard Dawkins'

'On the up side, the books from the closed libraries can be used to fuel the Town Hall furnace'

'Why does he have to keep dragging religion into it?'

'Our silences aren't awkward enough'

DUN
DUNNING

'Four across could be dog's bollocks'

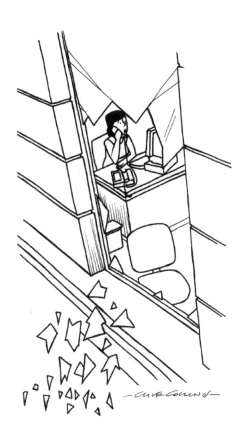

'I'm sorry – you've just missed him'

'Come on, counsel, sex it up a bit'

'I bet no two cornflakes are exactly the same, either'

'A sleep-over? I'll get my people
to talk to your people...'

'I'm not at my desk at the moment'

'Excuse me – I believe that is my seat'

'I remember you when you were this wide'

'They are... in no particular order...'

'Sorry, lads, you can't go in there without a tie'

'Your Rolex is also a fake'

'I'll say this for the recession –
it's given us a better class of beggar!'

'It's just... your father and I have decided to live apart. From you, that is'

'Congratulations, Nesbit'

'Nice to see you've got your old scowl back'

'We're going to claim imprisonment infringes your human rights to a family life'

'Darling! I've found another ingot'

'OK, put the golf clubs down real slooooww'

'That voice telling me to kill –
it was my satnav'

'They're out, this is the burglar speaking'

'No, no... come in... but you'll have to excuse the mess'

'I'm feeling a sense of conclusion here, so let's draw things to a close'

'Where the hell have you been? I was worried sick, I thought you'd been attacked'

'Share your innermost feelings or the remote gets it'

'Good book?'

'If you would like to join a support group for callers kept on hold, press 7...'

'Have you got any small ones?'

'Your babysitter's on the phone —
she wants to know how much she
should tip the fire brigade'

'Be about three hours'

'Is this water fattening?'

'Get rid of it, Horace, it's started to answer back'

'Today the bear is grizzly'

'Slow down, mind that rock, keep off the rough ground...'

D.I.Y. STORE
CUSTOMER SERVICE

FIND IT YOURSELF

'I urge the jury not to wreck the life of this young man, who has so recently bought his first tie...'

HOME WINE MAKING KIT

'They cannot be serious'

'Fancy an Indian?'

'I'm going to say a word, and you must say the
first thing that comes into your chest...'

'Do we do "ordinary"?'

'Which tie do you want to
wear – spinach, chicken and
gravy or oxtail soup?'

'Oh look, Mrs Hitchens from across
the road has come to see you'

'Ah, Janet, let me introduce Thomas – he's seen "The Sound of Music"
700 times. I'll leave you both together'

'It's not just a suit we're talking about here, Your Majesty.
It's a concept, a package for a lifestyle!'

EL
PRESIDENTE

'Remind me, do we pass the joint to the left or to the right?'

'The usual, Monsieur Henri?'

'The wolf you were trying to keep from
the door got in while you were out'

'Isn't it nice to see children walking to school?'

'Are you paying too much for
your car insurance?'

'Daddy had just one sleep-over too many'

'Time to get up and reinvent yourself'

'The sushi is totally authentic,
delivered to us in a Toyota van'

'George has been digitally remastered'

BILL PROUD

'I've found "just cause" on the internet!'

'I was a conscientious objector for people like you!'

'The name's Bond. Vagabond'

'9/11 has changed this conversation for ever'

'My husband particularly enjoyed the wine'

'And you're just a stone's throw
from the local school'

'And where are you going,
dressed to bore?'

BILL PROUD

'...and thanks to Guinness,
for sponsoring our holy vestments'

'I'd like a table where I can slurp my soup'

'And why do you think people take an instant dislike to you?'

'Worry lines – I like to see that in an employee'

'Settle out of court? Are you mad? I've just bought a new outfit'

'Once the pair have mated, the larger female spider devours the smaller, weaker male spider...'

'Let me know how you get on with these tablets – if they're any good I'll take them myself'

'Downshift or be downsized. The choice is yours...'

'So what's for dinner?'

'Someone should really take a look at that dripping tap in the gents'

'I heard you were available'

'I won't mince words with you, Mrs Norris – from now on you'll be setting one less place for dinner'

Okay, let's get married

'That's just the wine talking'

'Come up and see my tattoos, luv?'

It could catch on

'For your own personal safety, remote video monitoring is in operation while we play'

'They've developed a very sophisticated form of communication'

'Have you forgotten, Thompson, this is hair-shirt Thursday?'

'Not in front of the neighbours, dear'

'Oh, your people met my people all right.
Turns out they're the same people'

'Must do Munch'

'Whatever became of your plans for world domination?'

'Think of it this way – it's our money'

'Allowed to roam free? This chicken's had a better life than me!'

'...and our pamphlet, "101 Things To Do Whilst Waiting For a New Knee"'

'It's not just you, Bill. The whole darned department's gotta go'

St BLETHWENS SPORTS

'Could I have the contestants for the mummies' park-a-4x4 event?'

'No more for him – he's driving'

I've had more wives
than I've had hot dinners
Neither of them could
cook

'Doctor, please, put me out of my misery – kill my wife'

'There's something of the night
about you, Dennis'

'The trouble with this country is that all the people who know how to run it are too busy driving taxis or cutting hair'

'Let's sit still as little mice while James tells us about his alcohol problem'

'And you're gonna need a warning sign for that warning sign'

'You'll get up first thing in the morning and clean it all off'

'Remember, lads, next week: staff appraisals'

'Apparently Norfolk's the new Suffolk'

'Handing him the phone –
it never fails to stop him crying'

'Your son has headlice. Unfortunately, they
belong to a protected species'

'Well at least we've got you two talking'

'May I tell him why you're calling?'

'That's not how we summon
the Prince of Darkness'

'I wish he'd stand still, I want to
throw something at him'

'He's the local no-frills undertaker'

'I have this strange attraction to people who don't like me'

'Does it contain nuts?'

'In response to public pressure we're cancelling your bonus'

'You'll meet a tall, dark stranger online,
who will turn out to be a short,
fat ugly weirdo'

'Oh-oh. Here come the suits'

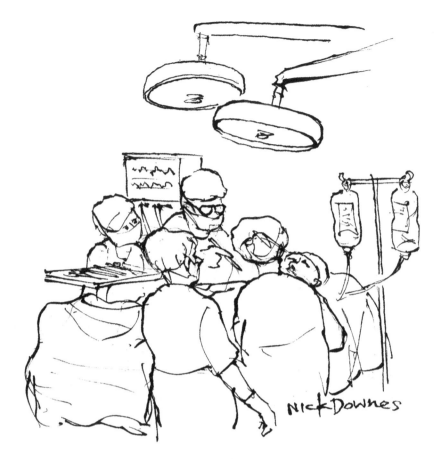

'Look at that poor excuse for a moustache'

'I'm not comfortable with this, Zog'

PARALYTIC GAMES

'Hang on, Gloria – I'm looking up their word for "inappropriate"'

WADDLIES!

'Hello – Mountain Rescue, I need some help with the ironing'

ENQUIRY

'Can you say why she crossed the road?'

'You've finally got the warts right but you still haven't captured that cheeky twinkle in my eye...'

'These days I do most of my shoplifting online...'

'I preferred his earlier work'

'Don't call me, text me, email me, visit my blog,
join me on Facebook or follow me on Twitter'

'Come on, Dad. You should make an effort to understand the new technology'

'Sorry. We'd like to try that again'

'Leave it out, woman, you're doing my head in!'

'If you begin to feel unwell,
start or stop taking aspirin...'

List of cartoonists included

A J Singleton
Aaron
Addison
Alexei Talimonov
BB
Beck
Bernie
Bill Proud
Blot
Bob
Bob Wilson
Burton
Caz
Chris Madden
Clive Collins
Cluff
Colin Wheeler
Colin Whittock
Cookson
de la Nougerede
Dish
Dredge
Feggo
Freiesleben
Ged
Generer
Geoff Horton
Geoff Thompson
Gf
Goddard
Gordon Gurvan
Grain
Grizelda Grizlingham
Holland
Hunter
Ian Baker
Ines

Ivor
Jacob
Jelliffe
Jonesy
Jorodo
K J Lamb
Ken Pyne
Kleh
KMS
Lawry
Len
Lowe
Mark Lewis
Marshall
Mazurke
McIntyre
McLachlan
McNeill
Meyrick Jones
Mico
Mike Turner
Mike Williams
NAF
Neil Bennett (NB)
Nick Baker
Nick Downes
Nick Hobart (Nick)
Pak
Pals
Paul Wood
Paulus
Pearsall
Philip Warner
R Lowry
Ray Jones
RGJ
Riach

Rich
Richard Tomas
Robert Thompson
Roger Latham
Royston
RR
Russell
Sally Artz
Sewell
Siobhan McCooey
Smith
Spittle
Steve Way
Stokoe
The Surreal McCoy
Tim Bales
Tony Husband
Warner
Waterhouse
Wilbur
Wren